MINGAN
my village

Poems by Innu Schoolchildren
Illustrated by Rogé
Translated by Solange Messier

FIFTH
HOUSE

Preface

One is never sure
of being human, which is to say

knowing friends
who march to the beat
of the hearts of children,
are guides
inspiring women

children of tradition
accept giving
words to their visions,
as if telling of dreams they've heard
and leaving their traces for you

JOSÉPHINE BACON

Foreword

Until recently, I had never had contact with First Nations people, except through their works of art. Their culture seemed inaccessible to me, almost exotic. It was through listening to Joséphine Bacon's poetry, through Chloé Sainte-Marie's songs, that the frontier opened to me. The sound of the Innu language resonated in me like a drum that carried me, not to a distant land, but to a familiar inner place; to a long-ago time to which I was somehow linked.

Perhaps I wanted to do this book to allow that place within myself to emerge, to reconnect with history; to allow myself to make this happen, to break the silence.

I went to Mingan, an Aboriginal reserve located on the North Shore, where students of the Teueikan school greeted me. I wanted to make a book of poetry with them for the pleasure of meeting them, but also to give them a forum to be heard. In this book, young Innu chose to transport us away from the difficulties and problems connected to their reality. Rather, their poems allow us to see the light that is behind their eyes—to bring us closer.

Through the Mingan children's writing, we can see the sun rise. Through their poetry, the children draw us forests to contemplate. They also build bridges, which I hope you will all cross.

Rogé

TO GILLES

Rogé

Listen to your heart
It speaks of our grandfathers
And our grandmothers

Sabrina

I hear the wind, breath of Teueikan
Pushing an eagle in the air

The clouds carry stories
Of snow and wind
Of sky and sun
Of moon and stars
Of rainbows and auroras
Borealis

The animals hide
Under fir trees
The dogs tell us:
"We want to come inside with you."
If I were a wolf in the forest
I would take refuge in a log

The ice breaks hard
A freezing fog
From the snow and the wind

When the storm blows
On the clouds, brilliant stories
In the blue sky

Pishumuss, Tiffany, Olivia, Séléna, Jeff, Karrianne

Camping
There where we pierce the winter's ice
To tighten the net
A new dream

Séléna

I think of the moose
Of the partridges and the trout
While I am in the forest
I walk barefoot in water as cold as snow
I dive in the lake
I swim with the thousands of fish

Devon

In the wind's light, the pain of the heart
The blue river
When I listen
I have a memory of my grandfather
He tells me he is well
This comforts me
I know he protects me
That he watches me
I cry when he is not beside me

Sabrina

When I hear the sounds of nature
It's like a song to me
It's your voice that I hear

Bradley

Nature is soft
The sky shines each day
When the leaves move
I think about the people who are in the sky
Nature is warm
In my eyes
Like water shining in the sun
And I listen to the bird that speaks to me
To me
And he tells me that my grandfather is well

Kitona

Climbing onto a white spruce
In front of the blue sky
I hear the gathering
The joy and the friendship
Amun of the summer

John-Dereck

It snows on the planets
When we walk on the sky

The stars flow like a river

Emmy

Nasha and Kukum Séléna watch the caribou. They want to kill it to nourish themselves, to create boots and clothing. But with no gun, they leave to request the help of Nimushum Pien. Once the three children return to the spot where they had seen the caribou, they realize it is no longer alone. She is accompanied by her baby. Kukum Séléna explains to Nasha that they will not kill the female caribou. Her baby needs her in order to grow up.

Shany, Daisy, Amanda, Alexane, Joshua, Maverick

There are beautiful things in my life
The green trees and the sky
Thousands of birds flying in the sky
Waterfalls with fish
The forest with its animals
Nature
When I listen to nature
It's like a very long song to me

Kaylène

When the eagle passes by us
We say that it's a spirit
Giving us a sign of love
Of friendship, goodness and courage
I imagine that the eagle is a truly sacred drum
When it passes by
When it flies in circles
When it flies up high

Our grandmothers
Our grandfathers
Pray to the eagle with tobacco or sage

Emmy

I don't know
Why the salmon exists…

Does it come from the heart of the Innu people
Where Utshekatak, the stars
Dance with Tshakapesh?
Does it come from the man on the moon
Who protects the Innu?

I don't know
Where the strength of the salmon comes from

Does it come from the Manitou River?
Does it come from Maikan, the wolf, its cousin
Or from inniun, life?

I don't know
Why the salmon resembles the sun
But I do know that once the cold pushes the clouds
And we warm up under the shaputuan
Uthashumek, the salmon
Gives us life

Cynthia, Maude, Derick, Gabriel, Émilie, Valère,
Raphaël, Thumah, Molly, Moïse, John-Dereck, Kakuss

While descending the Kuakuapishish River
I am transformed into a butterfly

With my new wings, like a wolf I cry
When night falls

Cynthia

Kimberley

When the ravens become white
I will stop loving you

Kimberley

Rogé and Éditions de la Bagnole would like to thank Laure Morali and Rita Mestokosho, poets and friends, who conducted the writing workshops and helped the children of Mingan to unveil their poet souls.

Laure presents Rita

Nomad

My feet desperately search to hang on
To the moss tundra
I fly with my soul
With the weightlessness of a cloud in the sky

RITA MESTOKOSHO

Rita Mestokosho, born in Mingan in 1966, published her first book, *Eshi Uapataman Nukum / How I See Life, Grandmother*, in 1995. This collection of poems has been translated in many languages and reedited in 2009 by Beijbom Books in Sweden with a preface by Jean-Marie Gustave Le Clézio (Nobel Prize for Literature, 2008) who wrote: "Rita's poetry speaks to us all, where we are in the world, regardless of origin or history. Rita's voice touches our hearts, because she is herself, without affectation, natural and clear." She also published her collection, *Uashtessiu / Lumière d'automne*, as a result of her fruitful correspondence with poet Jean Désy (Mémoire d'encrier, 2010).

Rita Mestokosho is the granddaughter of drummers Damien Mestokosho and Sylvestre Mollen and grand-niece of the great hunter, speaker and author of *tapashimuna*, Mathieu Mestokosho. She is the direct heiress of literature that is both poetic and epic; an old literature of at least seven millennia. She began to write at the age of thirteen in reaction to the silence of the elders, newly-settled nomads—the creation of the Ekuanitshit (Mingan) reserve took place in 1963, only three years before Rita's birth. With the power of words, she allows us to live the most subtle sensations of her grandparents' memories. Like a frozen river that can crack at any moment, Rita's poetry unleashes a force that threatens to make us stagger under the effect of a contained fragility. «My body is here, and my mind is there. I travel with the conviction that my speech is that of my ancestors and not a voice that is lost,» she told me.

Poetry allows her to give strength to the young by passing along the secrets she has pierced from the land of the elders. Her voice is similar to dreams of singing drummers who intone her melody to gather the clan in a circle during the dance of the makusham. Rita does not separate writing from life. She walks to the beat of her poems. And the circle widens until it contours the World.

Laure Morali

Rita presents Laure

Laure Morali, born in France in 1972, has published *La mer à la porte, La terre cet animal, La route des vents, La p'tite ourse* and *Traversée de l'Amérique dans les yeux d'un papillon* (Mémoire d'encrier, 2010). She is also the weaver of the collection of correspondence between Quebec writers and First Nations people, *Aimititau! Parlons-nous!* (Mémoire d'encrier, 2008). She gave her first poetry workshop in Mingan in 1996 and has never stopped passing on her passion for words. She lives in Montreal.

Children golden by snow wave at me, laughing under
the floating sheets of the blue sky. What is this village?
I must live it.
All morning I swim in a tide of laughter. The children
of Mingan give me joy that I have rarely known. It comes
from far away, perhaps the future.
The world has one flesh, one heart.

The road of the winds

LAURE MORALI

Laure Morali has a perspective on life that looks towards a horizon red in colour and black in ink. Blue allows her to dream of the sea no matter where she is. She writes with the Innu children to share with them her great love of life. It is the wind of the sea that has led her to Mingan, to us. Her journey begins each day with a blank sheet, while her heart beats and beats to find the quietude of northern rivers. She has slept on the moss of my ancestors in dreaming of a world where hatred does not exist. Laure Morali comes from the sea, where the islands find themselves with the stars during a July night. I have gotten to know Laure better every day, and one day never lasts long enough. She opens her heart to the children, because she sees childhood as a mirror. For her, hope has an invisible colour and poetry is a language without words. Her path is covered with flowers and large desert winters. She always returns to the sea, this woman of poetry. Guided by the force of destiny, she is still looking for an island where she can freely love the life that the Great Spirit has given her. She is a friend, a sister that I love.

Rita Mestokosho

Natuta tshitei
Uauineu tshimushuma
Uauineu tshukuma

E manikashinanuti
Anite tshe pakuanapanit
Anapit
ussi-puamunanu

Minuashu assi
Nanitam minu-tshishikau
E uepashtinikau nipisha
Nitshissituauat auenitshenat
uashkut ka tatau
Tshishiteu assi
Nimateniten nissishikut
Miam nipi e tishakamiteti usham
pishim(u)
Ninatutuau pineshish, nitaimik
Tshimushum minueniun nitik

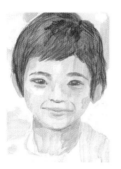

Nipeten nutin, teueikan uneneun
Uepauku mitshishua tshishikut

Kashkunat tipatshimeuat
Kuna, nutina
Pishimua kie uashkunu
Tipishkau-pishimua mak
utshekatikua
Mikupishana mak uashtushkua

Aueshishat kashuuat
Shek inashtit
Atimuat issishuat
Nuitshiuenan
Maikanuian
Pashkutshitikuat nipa kashun

Matueiashkatin mishkamit
Kashkunu, takaiau
Kunu mak nutin

E tshishkueienitakuaki
Kashkunit nukana tipatshimuna
E uasheshkuakui

Nitshissituauat mushat
Pineuat mak matamekush
Ka taian nutshimit
Nishashashtin tshetshi
pamikashian nipit e
tatshikamit miam kun
Nikutshin shakaikanit
Nameshat nuitsheukuat

Uapashitau kakatshuat
Apu tshika ut shatshitan

Tshikanakuan nutin
Tshikanakuan nutin,
tshikanakuan kassenitamun
Shipu uashekamu
Nitshissituau nimushum
Niminueniun nitik
kau ekue minuenitaman
Nitshissenimau ninakatuenimak
Niman eka etati pessish etaian

E natutaman assi
Nikamun nipeten
Tshipetatin

Minaikuat etanuti
Anite e uasheshkuat
Nipeten mamuitun
Minuenitamun mak
uitsheuakanitatun
Nipan amun

Mishpun
Pemutenanuti uashkut
Utshekatikuat
unashinataimuat shipunu

Nasha mak Kukum Séléna
tshitapameuat atikua. Ui
nipaieuat tshetshi mitishutau,
tshetshi

umassinitauat mak tshetshi
tutakau uteiunuaua. Apu
upassikanitau, nituapameuat
Nimushum Pien

tshetshi uitshikutau.
Tekushinitau nete ka
uapamatau apu peikussiniti,
utikussima uitsheukunua.

Kukum Séléna ekue itat
Nasha, apu tshika ut passuak,
utikussima eshk(u) tshika ui
nitautshinua.

Minashkuat
Minuashu nitiniun
Minashkuau mak uashku
Mishkashinakuashuat
pineshishat ishishikut
Nameshuna paushtikua
Aueshishat minuatamuat
minashkuat
E natutamani assi
Nikamun nipeten

Uiapamakaniti mitshishu
Manitu an itakanu
Tshuashtaimakanu e shatshitak
Menuitsheuanitatak, menuatatak
mak e shutshiteishkatak
Uiapamaki miam teueikan nitishi-
utinau
E pimipaniti
E tshinikuanaiki
E piminati
Tshimushuminuat
Tshukuminuat
Aiamitueuat Mitshishua e
patshitinimuatauat tshishtemaua

Apu tshissenitama
Tshekuan ma utshashumek(u) tat...
Anite a ututeu innit
Anite utshekatikuat
Anite ka nimit Tshakapesh
Innu ne ka tat tipishkau-pishimutat
Ka nakatuenimat innua?
Apu tshissenitaman
Tanite utshashumek(u) uetinak
ushutishiun
Anite a utinam(u) Manitu-shipit
Anite a utinam(u) maikanit,
ushteshikauna
Kie ma anite inniunit?
Apu tshissenitaman tshekuan ma
utshashumek(u) uet nishpatuat
pishimua
Muk(u) nitshisseniten tekati
uepashuat kashkunat
Tshetshi tshishutishiak(u)
shaputuanit
Utshashumek(u)
Tshiminukunnu tshitinniunanu

E maipaniani Kuakuapishish-shipu
Nikuakuapishiun
Nussi-utitakan miam tepuemakan
miam maikan e unuti
Tepishkaniti

*Thank you to the children of the Teueikan school in Mingan
for allowing me to photograph them and use their pictures to illustrate
the book: Uateshkuan Mestokosho-Rich, Tara Bellefleur-Napish,
Sharon Mestokosho, Paushtikuss Mestokosho-Rich, Nelly-Kim Washaulno,
Maverick Mollen-Mestokosho, Kaylène Mollen, Jordan Maloney-Benjamin,
Jessica Basile Napess and Etienne-Liam Rich.*

*Thank you also to Joséphine Bacon for the Innu translation of the poems and
Mr. Allen Ward, director of the Teueikan school for supporting the project.*

Rogé

English translation copyright © 2014, Fifth House Publishers

Originally published as *Mingan mon village*: © 2012,
Éditions de la Bagnole

Published in Canada by Fifth House Publishers,
195 Allstate Parkway, Markham, Ontario L3R 4T8

Published in the United States by Fifth House Publishers,
311 Washington Street, Brighton, Massachusetts 02135

10 9 8 7 6 5 4 3 2 1

Library and Archives Canada Cataloguing in Publication
Mingan my village
ISBN 978-1-92708-324-6 (Paperback)
Data available on file

Publisher Cataloging-in-Publication Data (U.S.)
Mingan my village
ISBN 978-1-92708-324-6 (Paperback)
Data available on file

Fifth House Publishers acknowledges with thanks the Canada Council
for the Arts, and the Ontario Arts Council for their support of our publishing
program. We acknowledge the financial support of the Government of Canada
through the Canada Book Fund (CBF) for our publishing activities.

Cover and interior design by Tanya Montini
Cover art courtesy of Rogé
Printed in China by Sheck Wah Tong Printing Press Ltd.